UNLOCKING YOUR

MONEY POWER

A guide to achieving wealth and financial freedom

WALTER HADERSON

All rights reserved. No part of this work may be duplicated, distributed, or communicated in any way, including photocopying, recording, or additional mechanical or electronic techniques, without the prior written permission of the publisher except in the case of brief quotations embodied in critical reviews and certain other noncommercial uses permitted by copyright laws.

Copyright © Walter Handerson, 2024.

DEDICATION

To God, for guiding me
And to
Victoria, for being a source of inspiration

Table of Contents

DEDICATION iii
INTRODUCTION vii
1 1
THE PSYCHOLOGY OF MONEY 1
2 10
MONEY AND EMOTIONS.................................. 10
3 20
INCOME, EXPENDITURE AND DEBT 20
4 34
SETTING CLEAR FINANCIAL GOALS.................. 34
5 50
INVESTMENT 50
6 63
LET YOUR ASSETS BUY YOUR LUXURIES 63
CONCLUSION.. 73
STAYING DETERMINED 73

INTRODUCTION

Welcome to "Unlocking your money power: A guide to achieving wealth and financial freedom" I am excited to embark on this transformative journey with you as we explore the keys to unlocking your money power and discover the path to true wealth and freedom.

In this book, we will lay the foundation for the incredible journey ahead we will begin by delving into the psychology of money and understanding its significance in our decisions. Money is not just a means of exchange; it provides us with the freedom to live life on our own terms, fulfill our dreams and holds the potential to shape our future.

Together we will define your personal financial goals, because without a clear destination in sight, it becomes challenging to navigate the path towards financial independence. We will discover how these goals are not merely about accumulating wealth but encompasses a broader vision of what you desire in life. By identifying and aligning your financial goals with your value and aspirations you will find the motivation and purpose necessary to propel you forward on this journey.

Remember, this book is not a magic formula for overnight success; it is a roadmap, a guide that will empower you to make informed decisions and take deliberate actions towards financial freedom. Your commitments, dedication and willingness to learn and apply these principles will be the driving force behind your success.

So let's dive in together and embark on this extraordinary adventure towards unlocking your financial freedom. By the end of this book you will have gained the knowledge, tools and mindset necessary to create a life of abundance, wealth and freedom.

Get ready to transform your relationship with money and embrace a future where financial constraints are a thing of the past.

1

THE PSYCHOLOGY OF MONEY

Everybody is wired differently. Our dreams, worries, and passions are not the same. Additionally, everyone experiences different ideas and feelings when they hear the word money. Knowing the psychology of money will make us more conscious of such feelings, ideas, and actions.

What is the psychology of money?

The study of how we behave with money is known as money psychology.

Financial success isn't determined by intelligence, knowledge, or math prowess. It's all about behavior, and everyone tends to do some things more than others. You can actually change your life once you recognize your inclinations and take control of your own mind, thoughts, and willpower.

I've been researching the psychology of money for the past ten years, and I've witnessed it in action. Because this material is so potent, I invite you to delve in with me.

The Significance of the Psychology of money

I've come to value self-awareness as a tool. If I desire to grow, I need to know more about how my mind functions. In order to make significant changes, knowing oneself is essential, whether the topic is money or life in general.

I adore personality tests because they bestow upon me the precious gift of self-awareness. Unaware of our own strengths, weaknesses, perceptions, and tendencies, we will never be able to guide ourselves toward improvement and the achievement of our financial objectives.

You must educate yourself on the psychology of money if you hope to understand the underlying causes of your actions, including why you save, spend, take on debt, put off investing, and more.

Four Ways psychology affects your money

I adore studying financial inclinations and the role money plays in a person's life. Everyone is unique, as I've previously stated, and none of these inclinations are good or bad. It's just how you're naturally wired. Here are four things I want you to discover in your money mindset

1. Spender vs. Saver

Most individuals find it very straightforward to decide if they're a spender or a saver. Spenders can see so many creative possibilities when it comes to money. This is completely me! Whenever I have extra money, it burns a hole in my pocket, and I can't wait to spend it.

On the other hand, a saver's first instinct is to not spend their money. They feel lot better about having money stowed away. Savers are patient and willing to wait to make a buy.

What's dangerous for spenders and savers both is going to the extremes. As a spender, if you spend everything you make, you're going to be broke. And ultimately, if you save everything you make, you're going to miss out on a lot of pleasant activities that offer joy to your life. This is quite evident when we think about it—but the point is that we need to think about it.

We think about it—but the point is that we need to think about it.

2. Free Spirit vs. Nerd

Are you familiar with the two categories of budgeters?

Nerds love to crunch numbers. They actually look forward to setting up their financial plan. Weirdoes. (Just kidding) Seeing where their money is going each month and coming up with new ideas to make it function even better makes them feel good. They adore how everything is organized and in its proper spot. Free spirits are..... Well, we are the party! We are able to enjoy life more because we are not overly preoccupied with the details. The categories for amusement and shopping are in essence your love language, but if you're a free spirit, the very mention of the word budget may make you break out in hives. Living life to the fullest is what free spirits enjoy!

Nerds require the free spirits to provide some entertainment value to the budget for non-essential expenses like birthday celebrations, trips, and date evenings.

The nerds are necessary to assist Free Spirits in creating a reasonable budget.

Before you believe that those who enjoy spending money are free spirits and those who are more prone to save money are nerds, think again. In reality, my dad is a nerd-spender. He enjoys spending money, but he also enjoys monitoring his spending.

3. Status vs. Safety

Which drives your financial motivation—status or safety? You might need to go through some serious private reflection for this one. Think about what drives you to save or spend money, and be honest with yourself. Making the psychology of money work for you depends on this this piece.

Safety-conscious people want the security that money can buy. People desire assurance that they can survive unexpected financial hardships, job loss, or even a medical calamity. Being a safety person means that you have to be careful not to live in fear. Fear can prevent you from investing for retirement, giving liberally, or even from buying new shoes when your daily pair is obviously worn out and needs to be replaced.

For those for whom money is a measure of success, then it is a status symbol. Their financial situation has an impact on the kind of house they live in, the activities they participate in, and their capacity to take that ideal holiday.

4. Your Upbringing and Family

Your attitude toward money was undoubtedly shaped from an early age by the way you heard your parents talk about it, or not talk about it. While it won't fully define your financial philosophy, knowing this will help.

Unlocking your money power

Here's an illustration of how financial disputes as an adult might result from past experiences: Do you become upset and even argue with your partner when they buy, say, the brown, organic, cage-free eggs? "It's just $2 more than the gross white ones," he protests. "That's $2 that could go toward something else!" you argue.

Have you ever wondered why you get so worked up about eggs that are organic? Is it because while growing up, your family's shopping budget was a source of stress? Or perhaps your parents scoffed at hippie-dippie, farm-to-table groceries? Perhaps you're a saver-safety person because you didn't have much growing up and, understandably, feel uneasy about spending extra on anything.

I'm not familiar with your history. Perhaps there's something else going on in your life besides a dozen eggs that's making money tense. Here's where self-awareness can result in healing, transformation, and unprecedented growth.

Walter Handerson

How Your Decisions Are Affected by the Psychology of Money

In actuality, money is really a magnifying glass that enhances your identity. Generosity and kindness will lead to even greater generosity and kindness when it comes to money. You'll be much more impolite and self-centered when it comes to money if you're unpleasant and conceited. Money is only a tool, and you have the freedom to decide how to use it.

The psychology of money influences hundreds of small decisions we make on a daily basis without even realizing it. I see the safety vs. status tendency as one example. I err on the side of status. A premium automobile or designer handbag will probably be valued more by me, and if making a greater purchase makes me feel successful in some manner, I'll probably be able to justify it.

One may argue that this simply indicates my preference for fine things, and believe me when I say that if you can afford them, there's nothing wrong with having lovely things. However, I have to control my spending because I am aware of my status propensity. I have to keep in mind that my possessions do not characterize who I am.

I am aware that this work is difficult, but you are capable. I've witnessed millions of people from various walks of life and financial situations muster the bravery to bring about long-lasting change for their whole family tree, so I know you can too! It's not simple. The good news is that you can start now and that it is achievable.

2

MONEY AND EMOTIONS

The relationship with money is one of the most complex that we encounter in our lives, entwined with not only societal influences but also our own personal growth and experiences as we grow and progress through life.

And, like any other important relationship, the one with money is deeply emotional.

We feel a specific way when we have or don't have money and when we believe we've spent too much or too little. These feelings influence how we behave in the future.

Money is frequently associated with a wide range of unpleasant, negative feelings, the most prominent of which include guilt, shame, envy, anxiety, and fear. However, it can also be associated with exceptionally intense, good sensations, such as a euphoric rush of delight when you have money and can treat yourself to, say, an expensive restaurant or vacation. Let's discuss a few of these.

Shame: This is the most common emotion associated with money. When we believe we have failed ourselves, we experience a sense of shame. This shame stems from preconceived expectations we may have placed on ourselves. You might have felt ashamed after spending more than you thought you should. Or maybe you made a comment along the lines of, "Am I making enough?" Are my savings enough? How do I plan for the future? Will I ever be able to have a good life? I wish I earned as much as "XYZ." I still can't afford to buy a house, while others have.

Guilt: Guilt differs from shame in that it arises from feeling undeserving of something, in this case financial wealth or health. For example,` if you have more money than your peers or if your parents are financially supporting you, you may experience shame, which may sometimes be detrimental to your personal sense of autonomy. You may also feel guilty after spending and depriving yourself of things in the future because you believe you do not deserve them owing to your previous lack of control. When will I quit getting money from my parents? I shouldn't buy anything good for myself this month because I already bought those pricey shoes last month.

Fear: Fear is another common emotion associated with money. Fear of not having enough may keep us in unsatisfactory work. Alternatively, the fear of not being accepted or belonging may drive us to pay more than we can afford to be with particular people or the fear of appearing ignorant, so you don't query the price of something in a store or question why something costs so much. It could also be a fear of inciting envy, so you avoid disclosing certain aspects of your life for fear of eliciting jealousy and judgment. Or the dread of asking for the money you truly deserve.

Greed and Envy: Wanting what others have is a basic human emotion, and money makes even the most cynical people envious. In most aspects of life, comparing oneself to others is a major source of dissatisfaction; this is also true when it comes to money. People are often evaluated by their financial status, and when we believe someone has more than us, we often assume they lead a better, more contented life, which can breed envy. Envy that we are unable to publicly express and accept might be rationalized by illogical competitiveness, misguided hatred, and baseless criticism. Despite her enormous wealth, she is incredibly foolish and conceited. They simply inherited all that money; they never worked a day in their lives. He merely works for his mother. It's not as though he is skilled.

The aforementioned instances are only a small sample of the various emotions that are common at various phases of life. We need to have this conversation about the emotional significance of money, because if we continue to ignore it, nothing will change in this relationship.

These kinds of emotional responses, particularly the shame-related one, can entail a dreadful sense of uneasiness. We put off "dealing with our finances" because it makes us feel stressed. We dread the thought of paying taxes because we believe we are incapable of managing our own finances. We may put it off for years in order to avoid the momentary anxiety that comes with seeing those scary envelopes.

Laziness and procrastination are common excuses for this lack of enthusiasm. However, over time, it starts a vicious cycle in which we continue to put off taking action in order to get a short-term fix, which exacerbates our general financial worries. Thus, over time, it merely gets worse and worse.

Money and upbringing

Now that we know that everyone has an emotional relationship with money, let's go a step further.

How did we come to feel this way about money?

Where do our feelings about it originate?

Like many other aspects of our lives, our upbringing has influenced our basic behavior and attitude toward money.

The way our parents or other family members approached money, their spending habits, and their mentality all had a big impact on how we handled our own wallets as adults.

If you were raised in a home where poverty was a factor, you may have developed a scarcity mindset as a result of your upbringing. This indicates that you're constantly concerned about running out.

Alternatively, having grown up in such a system may have made you more determined to alter the mindset of your family by putting in more effort or being unduly indulgent.

Our upbringing and how we handle our personal finances as adults are greatly influenced by our parents' financial philosophy, our family's inheritance, and the positive and negative roles that our extended family plays in society. There may be an underlying drive within you to earn at least as much as your parents or the obligation to handle the family's inheritance in the purportedly proper manner.

Money as a Mindset

The one benefit of having an emotional attachment to something is that feelings are excellent markers. When we have a reliable indicator, we may take concrete action to address the issues they are highlighting. And they typically appeal to beliefs when they do this.

Beliefs are ideas that we harbor throughout our lives. And everything we've internalized throughout the years fertilizes these.

Developing a deeper understanding of and ultimately improving our connection with money can be achieved by fully utilizing these feelings.

Identifying your feelings, exploring them further, and shedding light on the underlying assumptions that cause them can all help you have a better relationship with money.

Analyzing these beliefs might assist or determine whether they are still applicable to your current circumstances or if they are merely inherited ideas from your family. Maybe you no longer have the same beliefs that you did at one point in your life, but you still act as though they still apply when it comes to making financial decisions. Maybe it's time to let go of it.

Perhaps you've learned that riches should be kept concealed, that wealthy people are terrible, or that money should be preserved rather than squandered or that you ought to save every cent and refrain from indulging yourself.

As a result, developing a better connection with money and gradually changing views can be facilitated by purposefully being conscious of emotions.

This can help you make more thoughtful financial decisions by allowing you to ask yourself things like, ***"What is my money*** *for?" Where do my beliefs originate? Are they still applicable? How does spending money make me feel better?*

Once you've reached this level of introspection, you may be able to change your perspective and attempt to look at money from a different angle. You might change your perception of what your financial position looks like by using it as a motivational issue. It can be viewed as a way to share support, have experiences, or just to just love yourself back.

You can go from thinking, "I just spent too much on that restaurant," to thinking, "That was a wonderful meal that I deserve," by bringing your values to the forefront of your conscious awareness. I should keep in mind that I work for money in order to eventually satisfy myself.

The most important thing to keep in mind is that changing your relationship with money begins with your thinking. Recognizing that financial stress is ingrained in people, but forcing yourself to face the issue head-on is the first step towards making the change.

Delaying handling financial matters such as taxes, budgeting, and being aware of your personal finances by actively monitoring your bank account can significantly lessen the long-term stress we accumulate due to money.

Financial transparency-generating solutions can help facilitate this. Knowing where your money is moving over time can provide reassuring clarity on potential areas for savings. Or it could make them more approachable (though they might not become pleasant, we won't lie!) once you learn how your taxes actually operate and what you can do to maximize them.

You might be able to establish more reasonable financial objectives if you have greater clarity because you will know where your money is going. Furthermore, you have greater power over your finances the more informed you are.

It's not simple for everybody. Usually, it's a significant change.

It's intimidating at first, sometimes even overpowering. However, money becomes less frightening the more you understand how it operates.

Unlocking your money power

Participating in your relationship with money, as with any other significant relationship in life, can help to simplify it, eliminate obstacles and traumas, and ultimately transform it into a more fulfilling and healthy relationship that will grow with you.

Hey, keep in mind that money is ultimately a social construct as well, so you can make of it what you will.

3

INCOME, EXPENDITURE AND DEBT

What is income?

The primary source of income for those in the workforce is their regular salary or wages. In the business world, income is the amount of money left over after all costs and taxes are paid from the core operation.

All things considered, income is just what someone earns over time. There are two categories of income: taxable income and non-taxable income, according to the income tax department.

What are the different types of income?

As a superpower country, the United States of America creates millions of new job opportunities annually. It is also extremely varied in a lot of ways.

The same holds true for the different kinds of enterprises, jobs, and revenue streams. There are five categories of income from the standpoint of income taxes:

- ✓ Salary head
- ✓ House property
- ✓ Gains and profits from a career and business (PGPB)
- ✓ Capital gains
- ✓ Other sources

These are the various categories or heads of revenue sources in a broad format. These are the main sources from which people obtain their living resources.

- The first category under income tax is salary, which covers such fundamentals as comprehending all compensation that an individual receives for services rendered to the company under the terms of an employment contract.

- Income from house property is the second head of the income tax. The guidelines for determining an individual's total principal income from their home or land are contained in Sections 22 through 27 of the Income Tax Act of 1961.

- Income from Profits of Business is the third income tax head. Under this head, the total income is calculated using the income from business or professional profits.

- Profits or gains realized by the holder through the sale or transfer of any capital assets that were held as investments are referred to as capital gains. Capital gains are any assets that a holder holds for their business or profession.

Any additional source of income that isn't included in the aforementioned headings can be categorized under this heading. This category includes interest income from bank deposits, winnings from lotteries, card games, gambling, and other sports awards.

Expenditure

Taking charge of your financial destiny is at the heart of personal expenditure management, which goes beyond simply keeping track of your spending. Consider your spending patterns to be an expression of your objectives and top priorities. A life free of stress and more fulfillments can result from mastering them. However, where do you even begin?

Let's start by discussing budgeting. Your financial path is your budget. It helps you prepare for savings and outlines your income and expenses. Though it may seem difficult, making a budget is actually easier than you might imagine. List all of your sources of income first. Next, group your expenditures. While discretionary expenditure, such as eating out, entertainment, and shopping, allows greater flexibility, fixed expenses, such as rent, utilities, and loan payments, are non-negotiable.

The 50/30/20 rule is one useful tactic. Set aside 50% of your income for needs, 30% for wants, and 20% for debt reduction and savings. This rule makes sure you take care of the necessities while having fun and making plans for the future.

Unlocking your money power

Maintaining a spending diary is essential. To keep track of your spending, use tools like spreadsheets and budgeting applications. You can spot trends and make changes by doing this. Perhaps you were unaware of the total cost of those daily cups of coffee. Over time, little adjustments might have a significant impact.

Next, arrange your expenses by priority. Find out what matters most to you. Are you merely enjoying in transient pleasures or are you investing in experiences that enhance your life? Spending in a way that is consistent with your principles can make you happier. For example, if you value travel, reduce the amount of stuff you buy and put money aside for your ideal trip.

Even the greatest budget can be derailed by impulsive purchases. Use the 24-hour rule to your advantage by delaying non-essential purchases by one day. The impulse will usually subside, and you won't experience buyer's regret. In addition, refrain from opening online stores out of boredom and unsubscribe from marketing mailings.

Management of debt is still another important factor. Credit card debt and other high-interest debt may become out of control very rapidly. Prioritize paying off these bills. Think about the snowball technique (paying off the smallest bills first for psychological incentive) or the avalanche method (paying off the highest interest rate loans first). Pick the one that best fits you; both offer advantages.

Another top objective should be saving money. The emergency fund should be able to cover three to six months' worth of living expenditures. This safety net offers financial security and peace of mind in the event of unforeseen circumstances such as job loss or medical issues. To maintain consistency, automate your savings.

Investing is an additional means of increasing your money. Invest first in retirement accounts such as an IRA or 401(k), particularly if your employer matches your contributions. Compound interest has the power to greatly grow your money over time. Think about varied investments as well, such as real estate or index funds.

Unlocking your money power

Finally, never stop learning about personal finances. To keep updated, read books, listen to podcasts, and follow financial gurus. Your ability to make wiser decisions increases with knowledge.

To put it briefly, managing personal expenses entails setting up a budget, keeping tabs on expenses, setting priorities for purchases, handling debt, carefully saving money, and making prudent investments. By forming these routines, you can live a more secure and contented life and become financially independent. Recall that making conscious decisions that align with your values and goals is more important than depriving yourself.

What is Debt?

To put it simply, debt is the sum that a borrower owes to a lender. A debt is an amount of money borrowed for a specific length of time that must be paid back, with interest.

Tips and strategies for handling debt

The majority of us will deal with debt at some point in our lives. It can manifest itself in a variety of ways, including credit card debt, mortgages, auto loans, and student loans. While taking on debt is frequently required for large life investments, if it is not handled well, it can also be a tremendous burden. Financial stress and misery can result from debt that rapidly gets out of control if careful planning and action aren't taken. Here are some pointers and methods for handling debt with personal checking accounts and other crucial money instruments.

In order to preserve stability and good financial health, effective debt management is essential. It entails keeping track of and managing your debts, making sure that payments are made on time, and choosing wisely when to borrow money and repay it. You may avoid late fines, excessive interest charges, and credit score harm by managing your debt effectively. Knowing that your financial obligations are in control also brings peace of mind.

Opportunities in the future can arise from effective debt management. Better interest rates on credit cards and loans can result from having a clean credit history, potentially saving you hundreds of dollars over time.

When bills arrive, pay them.

Paying your invoices as soon as they arrive is one of the simplest yet most effective debt management techniques. This lessens the possibility of forgetting to make a payment and paying interest or late penalties.

Making debt payments a priority

Not every debt is made equally. Interest rates and penalties for nonpayment vary depending on the type of debt. As a result, in order to efficiently manage your debts, you must prioritize them.

High-interest loans should usually be paid off first because their total cost increases over time. The 'avalanche' method of debt repayment is when you pay off the loans with the highest interest rates first and only make the minimum payments on the remaining loans.

Always make the minimum payment.

Make sure you always pay the minimum amount owed on all of your debts each month, regardless of your debt repayment plan. If you don't, you risk paying late fees, higher interest rates, and a lower credit score. Making the minimum payment demonstrates to lenders that you are devoted to fulfilling your financial obligations, even if you are unable to pay off a debt in full.

Keep in mind that the minimum payment is all that it is: the minimum. While paying the minimum amount due will maintain the good standing of your account, it will not significantly lower the principal amount owed.

Compile a list of everything You Owe.

It's critical to grasp your financial responsibilities in order to manage your debt successfully. Make a list of all the things you owe first. Included in this is a list of all the loans you have outstanding, including credit card balances, mortgages, auto loans, school loans, and any other liabilities.

Make a note of each debt's total amount owed, interest rate, minimum payment required, and due date. This thorough summary will provide you a quick picture of your financial condition and assist you in setting priorities for your debt reduction.

Establish an Emergency Fund to Prevent Needless Debt

Creating an emergency fund is a crucial first step in debt management. Life is full with unexpected expenses, such as medical bills, auto repairs, or sudden job loss. Without an emergency fund, you may be compelled to rely on credit cards or loans to cover these bills, resulting to extra debt.

Strive to save three to six months' worth of living expenses in an easily accessible emergency fund. Start by setting aside a little amount of your salary each month and progressively expand your savings over time.

Pay What You Can Really Afford

When managing your debt, it's vital to pay what you can genuinely afford rather than just the minimal payments. While minimum payments keep your accounts in good standing, they sometimes just cover the interest rates, leaving the principal balance unchanged.

How to Rebuild Your Credit after Debt Issues

If you've faced debt troubles in the past that have negatively impacted your credit score, it's crucial to take actions to rebuild your credit. Here are some strategies to consider:

- Make timely payments.
- Cut back on the amount of credit you use.
- Spread out your credit.
- Limit the number of fresh credit applications you submit.
- Make use of credit builder loans or secured credit cards.

4

SETTING CLEAR FINANCIAL GOALS

Do you feel that despite your best efforts, you are never able to succeed in making wise financial decisions? Or have you been working so hard, perhaps even starting a side business, but at the end of the month, you don't have much to show for it?

Yes, real-life events like recessions and inflation might feel like major obstacles to achieving your financial objectives. But even in times when the economy isn't collapsing, you'll undoubtedly feel stuck if you don't have any financial goals.

Setting financial objectives is necessary if you want to actually advance with your finances. But try not to panic. I'm going to assist you in identifying your true financial objectives and provide you with the steps necessary to achieve them. You can succeed at this!

What is a financial goal?

A financial goal is any money-related plan you have. Both short and long term financial goals are acceptable (e.g., saving $1,000 for a down payment on a property or investing for retirement). Although having objectives for every aspect of your life is a good idea, setting financial goals demonstrates your commitment to your desires by outlining how you will save and spend money to achieve them.

But depending on how you feel about money, figuring out what to do with it may be as exhilarating or as intimidating as picking what to watch on Netflix or booking a trip to Disneyland. There's an abundance of choices. However, you are unable to ride every ride or watch every house remodeling program simultaneously. You must make your own decisions, and I advise addressing your objectives in a way that will position you for long-term success. Let's start by discussing how to adopt a goal-setting mindset.

Six steps to setting financial goals

Your financial objectives can be influenced by a variety of factors, such as your future aspirations, values, and motives. Your own spending and saving habits, as well as the way your parents managed money, have a significant influence on how you manage money.

Setting goals requires self-awareness and intention, so set aside some time to consider your objectives. Set aside some time to enjoy a glass of wine or a cup of coffee, and prepare to dream big! You're prepared to divide your financial goals into more manageable chunks after you've made a list of them. Here's how to do it:

1. Make your goal specific

People's financial goals are often unmet because they are overly ambiguous. "I want to be better with money," one may claim, but what does that actually mean to you? Put a greater emphasis on it or you say "Someday, I want to upgrade my car." Okay, enjoy yourself! But whatever kind of vehicle are you looking for and when are you hoping to get it?

What if you made the decision to pay off your debt instead? That's a particular region you should allocate funds for. Let's now discuss how to further deconstruct this objective.

2. Let your goal be measurable

All right, so you want to pay off your debt. It's time to choose a precise figure now, something you can gauge to see if you achieved your objective or not.

Although being totally debt-free ought to be your ultimate objective, it's a good idea to divide that goal into more manageable parts. In this manner, before you begin, you may see where you want to go.

Let's say that your entire debt is $30,000. Paying off your smallest debt, such as a $15,000 school loan, should be your first priority. By setting a measurable goal, I mean just that.

Walter Handerson

3. Set a deadline for yourself.

Here's the thing: If your goals don't have a deadline, it's quite simple to put them off. Give up promising to start eventually. You must set an acceptable deadline for yourself that is also a little difficult.

Resuming the example of the student loan: When do you hope to achieve your objective? You will need to spend $1,250 a month if you wish to pay off $15,000 in a year. Is this both feasible and a little bit unrealistic? Good if that's the case!

Some goals however, are short to mid-term in nature and can be completed in less than five years. Consider long-term objectives as ones you want to accomplish in at least five years. These are a few instances of both short- and long-term financial objectives:

Short and mid-term financial goals:
- Saving cash for emergencies
- Putting money aside for a trip
- Purchasing textbooks for a forthcoming academic term
- Investing in remodeling or a new kitchen appliance
- Putting money aside for an engagement ring
- Making a down payment on a lease for an apartment
- Putting money aside for future dental or medical needs

- Purchasing presents for Christmas or birthdays
- Savings for a down payment on a home

Long-term financial goals:
- Cash-only purchase of a new vehicle
- Making financial payments for your child's college
- Putting money aside for retirement
- Starting a company
- Spending several months at a time traveling

4. **Ensure that they are your own goals**

We are always losing the game we play when we compare ourselves to other people. Thus, be sure that the financial objectives you set are appropriate for you. Put another way, you shouldn't remodel your kitchen just because all of your friends are taking out second mortgages to do so. Is that one instagram influencer going on yet another lavish trip? Well done, guys. However, this does not imply that you have to follow suit or that you are falling behind if you are not in the same area. Keep your head down, concentrate on your objectives, and stay in your lane. And be explicit about the reasons behind your goal selection.

5. Put your goals in writing

Are you aware that putting your goals in writing increases your chance of succeeding? Yes, it is true that writing things down makes you more likely to stick with the task at hand.

So go ahead and put your objectives in writing. After that, place them on your desk, in your car, or on the mirror in your restroom. Put them in your phone's notes app, snap a picture of it, and set it as your wallpaper so that when you pick up your phone, it will be the first thing you see. Maintaining your objectives in plain sight will help you stay motivated and on course.

6. Get a goal accountability buddy.

Locate a goal accountability partner to help you reach your objectives further. it can be your partner, a close friend, or members of the community—anyone who will support and encourage you while you continue to strive toward achieving your objective. When you strive for your objectives, it can be really empowering to know you're not alone and to have someone rooting for you

Five Examples of financial goals

It can be difficult to know which financial objectives you should prioritize when there is so much financial "advice" flying around. For this reason, whenever I discuss creating financial objectives, I have to bring up the Baby Steps. You can pay off debt, accumulate wealth, and save for emergencies using the "Baby Steps." But there's a procedure to adhere to.

Is it better to pay off debt first? Set aside money for your kid's college education? Purchase a home? Invest in your golden years? The 7 Baby Steps provide you with a clear path to accomplish all those tasks by slicing through all the uncertainty. By following the stages, you'll be able to concentrate on one objective at a time, increase your financial success, and experience financial tranquility.

Here are some more of the most popular financial objectives that people set, along with advice on how to achieve them. Which ones are on your list?

Unlocking your money power

1. Create and stick to a budget.

Not only is budgeting one of the most popular financial decisions made every year, but it should also serve as the cornerstone for all other financial objectives.

Making progress with your money is possible with a budget. It's a budget that tracks your income and expenditures for both costs and income. Rather than wondering where your money went, you're telling it where to go. You can be certain that you're moving closer to your objective each month when you have this financial strategy in place.

Creating a budget gives you financial momentum in all areas.

2. Create an emergency savings account.

Life happens. However, if you have enough money saved up, you can be ready for any financial challenges that may arise. I am referring to medical bills, broken toilets, and car problems—you know, some of the most inconvenient aspects of growing up. However, having an emergency fund allows you to sleep soundly at night knowing that you won't have to take on debt to pay for those unexpected expenses.

To begin with, set a financial goal of saving $1,000. Then, it's time to pay off whatever debt you may owe. (I'll elaborate on that in a moment.) Following that, you should accumulate three to six months' worth of spending in an emergency fund. (Once more, the Baby Steps is a tried-and-true strategy that will assist you in taking charge of your finances.)

Having an emergency fund means you're prepared for those "life happens" situations. You won't have to worry about what might occur next since you will know that you have money saved up to handle it.

3. Pay off your debts.

It's time to take your debt repayment seriously if you have any. Yes, I am aware that it can appear unachievable at the moment, particularly if you're looking at some large debt figures like credit card debt, student loans, or other debt. The unpleasant reality is that debt doesn't help you advance. It prevents you from moving forward. If your money is continuously going into loan payments, you can't succeed financially.

4. Build up your retirement funds

For a moment, let's put on our thinking caps and visualize the perfect retirement. Perhaps that will happen in five, ten, or thirty years. Would you like to take the grandchildren and make a Disney trip every Christmas? Once every three months, take your spouse to a new state? Read every book on your shelf while lounging at home? Take up a nice pastime or go abroad to learn how to cook?

Your dreams for the future can come true only if you start making wise retirement investments today. Once your emergency fund is fully stocked and you are debt free, I want you to start setting aside 15% of your household income for retirement. And what do you know? All of the money you were paying on payments can go directly into your accounts to finance your retirement goals when you have no debt.

5. Reduce your spending and increase your savings.

Many individuals make vague objectives like "I want to save more money" or "I want to spend less money," but they rarely consider what it would really take to fulfill those desires. Folks, you need to be deliberate about your financial habits and precise about your ambitions.

Unlocking your money power

More than anything else, altering your behavior is the key to financial success. This can take the form of setting up and adhering to a monthly budget, shopping around, using coupons, paying with cash, or earning extra money. Here's a really important one: you have to develop the ability to say no, even to yourself. Not that I advocate never having fun. However, saving money will require some preparation and a change in lifestyle.

Lastly, here's one of my best advices for cutting costs and increasing savings: **Make a meal plan.** Meal planning helps you control your spending on food, which is where most of us go overboard.

Walter Handerson

Why Is Setting Financial Goals Important?

Setting financial goals enables you to focus more on the future. You'll begin to realize that every choice you make has an impact on your overall financial situation.

For instance, buying coffee and breakfast every day is not a huge deal if you don't have any financial objectives. But let's examine the true cost to you of that. For one workweek's worth of lattes, you'll usually spend at least $25, or $100 monthly! With that money, what other things could you do?

Compound growth can grow your $100 monthly investment into over $8,000 if you put it into an investment account for five years. You're drinking for an entire semester of your children's college education.

Consider investing $100 a month for 15 years—a much longer time frame—at a rate of 100 percent. Your savings on lattes could reach more than $45,000.

Unlocking your money power

And what if you spend thirty years investing your savings? You could end up with over $280,000 in coffee money. A daily cappuccino or a quarter of a million bucks? I enjoy a decent cup of coffee, but not that much, you guys.

Choose a small (or big) sacrifice you can make today to put yourself in a secure financial position. There is no doubt that the daily financial decisions you make today will have an impact on your future.

5

INVESTMENT

What is Investment?

In essence, an investment is an asset created with the intention of increasing financial growth. The wealth generated can be used toward a range of goals, including bridging income gaps, accumulating funds for retirement, or meeting particular obligations like loan repayment, tuition payment, or asset acquisition.

It's important to understand what an investment is because it can be challenging to select the right instruments at times to achieve your financial objectives. Making the appropriate decisions will be possible if you understand what an investment means in your specific financial situation.

You can earn income from investments in two different ways. One is that you could profit from your investment if you make it in a sellable asset. Second, you will generate income through the accumulation of gains if you invest in a plan that generates returns. Putting your savings into items or assets that increase in value over time or that will eventually contribute to income generation is the essence of investing, according to this interpretation of the term "investment."

Types of Investment

Investments can be made in stocks, bonds, mutual funds, exchange-traded funds (ETFs), index funds, and options, among other things. Check out the ones that might suit you. You have a lot of options as an investor as to where you should invest your money. It's crucial to carefully consider the various investment options.

Generally speaking, investments fall into three main categories: stocks, bonds, and cash equivalents. Within each bucket are numerous investment categories.

The following lists the six investment categories you should be aware of in order to achieve long-term growth. Note: Since money markets, certificates of deposit, and savings accounts are more about protecting your money than they are about growing it, we won't get into cash equivalents.

Six categories of financial investments
1. Stocks
2. Bonds
3. Mutual investment vehicles
4. Index funds

5. Options for Exchange-Traded Funds (ETFs)
6. Options

Stocks

An investment in a particular company is a stock. Buying stock is equivalent to purchasing a tiny portion of the assets and earnings of the company. To raise money, companies sell stock in their companies, which investors can then buy and sell amongst themselves. While stocks can yield large returns, they also carry a higher risk than other types of investments. Businesses may become worthless or cease operations.

How investors make money: When the value of the stock they own increases and they are able to sell it for a profit, stock investors profit. Additionally, some stocks give investors dividends, which are consistent payouts of a company's profits.

Bonds

A bond is a loan that you make to the government or business. You allow the bond issuer to borrow your money and repay it to you with interest when you purchase a bond.

Bonds are typically seen as less risky than stocks, despite the possibility that they will yield lower returns. The primary risk, similar to any loan, is that the issuer may cease making payments. Because U.S. government bonds are guaranteed by the country's "full faith and credit," this risk is essentially eliminated. Corporate bonds are typically regarded as the least hazardous option, with state and local government bonds coming in second. In general, the interest rate decreases with the riskiness of the bond.

Bonds are a fixed-income investment since investors anticipate regular income payments, which is how investors make money. Investors typically receive interest payments in installments of once or twice a year, with the entire principal amount due when the bond matures.

Mutual funds

You're not the only one who finds it difficult to select individual stocks and bonds. Actually, there's an investment designed just for people like you: the mutual fund.

Investors can buy a lot of different investments with mutual funds in one transaction. These funds combine the funds of numerous investors, and then hire a qualified manager to allocate the funds among stocks, bonds, and other assets.

Mutual funds operate according to a predetermined plan; for example, a fund may invest in foreign stocks or government bonds. Certain funds make investments in bonds and stocks. The investments made by the fund will determine how risky the mutual fund is.

How investors make profit: A mutual fund distributes a portion of its earnings to investors, such as stock dividends or bond interest. The fund's value grows in tandem with the value of the investments it holds, so you may be able to sell it for a profit. Keep in mind that purchasing a mutual fund requires paying an annual charge called the expense ratio.

Index funds

An index fund is a type of mutual fund that passively monitors an index instead of paying a manager to choose assets. To mimic the performance of the S&P 500, an S&P 500 index fund, for example, would own the equities of the index companies.

Index funds have the advantage of typically being less expensive due to the lack of an active manager on staff. An index fund's risk will vary according to the investments made inside the fund.

How investors make profit: Interest or dividends earned by index funds are paid to investors. Additionally, the value of these funds may increase in tandem with the benchmark indexes they track, allowing investors to profitably sell their fund shares. Expense ratios apply to index funds as well, but as was already mentioned, these expenses are typically less than those of mutual funds.

Exchange traded funds

ETFs are a kind of index fund that mimic the performance of a benchmark index by tracking it. Because they are not actively managed, they are typically less expensive than mutual funds, much like index funds.

The method by which ETFs are bought is the primary distinction between index funds and ETFs: Like stocks, they are traded on an exchange, so you can buy and sell ETFs at any time of day, and their price will change. Contrarily, the price of mutual funds and index funds is fixed at the end of each trading day and remains the same regardless of when you buy or sell. In summary, many investors may not care about this distinction, but if you would like greater control over the fund's price, an ETF may be more to your liking.

How investors make profit: Investing in mutual funds and index funds, for example, entails hoping that the fund's value will rise and you can sell it for a profit. Investors may also receive dividends and interest payments from ETFs.

Options

A contract to buy or sell stocks at a predetermined price by a predetermined date is called an option. Since the contract doesn't really require you to buy or sell the stock, options offer flexibility.

As the name suggests, this is a choice. Most options contracts include coverage for 100 shares of stock.

Purchasing an option entails purchasing the contract rather than the stock. At that point, you have three options: sell the options contract to another investor, let the contract expire, or buy or sell the stock at the agreed-upon price within the agreed-upon time frame.

How investors make profit: Although options can be extremely complicated, at their most basic, they allow you to lock in the price of a stock that you anticipate rising in value. You stand to gain from paying less for the stock if your crystal ball is correct. You can return the item and only lose the cost of the contract if it is incorrect.

Things to consider before investing

Putting money into investments could be a smart strategy to help you accumulate wealth over time.

Given the variety of options available, you don't need to be an expert in finance to succeed at it, even though it can occasionally seem overwhelming.

However, in the words of Warren Buffet, "not knowing what you're doing comes with risks, so it's important to understand the fundamentals.

Here are some things you should think about before investing to help you be more prepared and possibly lower your risk.

1. Set definite financial goals

Consider making a plan before making an investment. This aids in putting your investment objectives, as well as the timing and method of achieving them, into perspective. Eliminating the possibility of emotions impacting your investment choices can also be beneficial.

To begin, ask yourself what you hope to accomplish with your investments. Are you trying to save for a down payment on a home, increase your wealth for retirement, or pay for your child's education? Your investing strategy and the amount of risk you are willing to take can be influenced by your goals.

2. Evaluate your tolerance for risk and time frame.

It's crucial to think about how much risk you're willing to take on and how long you're willing to give yourself to reach your financial goal before making an investment.

For instance, a much younger person may have a very different investment plan for retirement. A less risky investment strategy may be more advantageous if you intend to access your money sooner rather than later and are unlikely to stay invested through market ups and downs.

3. Investigate the market

Before you consider investing, it's important to take the time to investigate what factors might have an impact on your investments so you can make informed decisions.

It's critical to comprehend both domestic and international market developments since they could affect your investment portfolio. This can include variables like inflation, interest rates, growth, unemployment, and even political developments.

4. Examine your feelings

It's undeniable that investing has an emotional component. Sometimes you might be tempted to alter your investing approach because a particular portion of your portfolio is struggling or you've heard recent news that the market is going to crash.

Even though these occurrences might make you act swiftly, selling off assets, it's still crucial to think through your investment plan. Making decisions based on transient market fluctuations can have a significant impact on your long-term strategy and the goals you have set for yourself which is something to consider, prior to making an investment.

5. Think about where to put your money.
Think about where you want to invest your money before making a purchase. You have the option of investing your money in a single asset class, like a residential property, or you can spread it out among several asset classes, like cash, bonds, and shares.

6. The act of diversification
You can diversify your risk by investing in a variety of asset classes, which is one of the main benefits.

This implies that your losses may not be as great if one of your investments underperforms because the other investments will help to offset the loss. However, it does require more work because you have to stay current in a number of market sectors.

6

LET YOUR ASSETS BUY YOUR LUXURIES

What are assets?

Assets are valuable things that have the potential to increase in value over time or produce income. This includes investments in stocks, bonds, property, businesses, and even intellectual property. Liabilities use up your resources, whereas assets provide you with passive income. The goal is to amass a collection of assets that will yield enough income to support your wants and indulgences.

Types of assets

Every kind of asset has a distinct function and can improve a person's financial situation or a company's ability to operate. Achieving long-term financial goals, investment strategies, and financial planning all depend on knowing how to leverage these assets efficiently.

1. Tangible Assets

Physical assets that have a tangible presence and can be felt or seen are known as tangible assets. Because of their physical characteristics, they have inherent value.

Theory: Let's say you are the proprietor of a small construction firm. Heavy machinery used in construction, like bulldozers and excavators, is one of your tangible assets. These resources are necessary for your building endeavors. They help you complete projects successfully and bring in money for your company by enabling you to carry out jobs like moving dirt and excavating foundations with efficiency.

2. Financial Assets

Intangible assets that stand in for a claim to future cash flows or financial advantages are known as financial assets. They derive their worth from either ownership rights or contractual claims.

Theory: You choose to purchase government-issued bonds. Because you can expect to receive interest payments on a regular basis and have your bond's face value returned when it matures, these bonds are considered financial assets. Your entire financial portfolio is improved by the consistent income stream from interest payments you receive from holding these assets.

3. Investment Assets

Assets held primarily for the aim of earning a return on investment are known as investment assets. They are bought with the hope of increasing their value or producing income.

Suppose you make investments in a diverse portfolio of mutual funds and stocks. The purpose of selecting these investment assets is to meet long-term financial objectives. You gain from capital appreciation as your investments increase over time, and if any of the stocks you own pay dividends, you may also get paid on a regular basis. These assets are useful because they have the potential to increase in value and generate income.

4. Fixed Assets (PP&E: Property, Plant, and Equipment)

In corporate operations, fixed assets, sometimes referred to as PP&E, are long-term tangible assets. They are not meant for resale and have a useful life of multiple accounting periods.

Theory: manufacturing company possesses specialized machinery and a factory building. The production processes of the company rely heavily on these fixed assets. The facility provides space for manufacturing, and the machinery enables efficient output. These resources support the business's capacity to supply goods to clients and turn a profit.

6. Intangible Assets:

Although they are not physical, intangible assets are nonetheless valuable. They can include contractual rights, brand awareness, and intellectual property. Generally, they are non-monetary.

Theory: A tech business has patents for creative software solutions. The intellectual property of the business is represented by these intangible assets. They give the business the only authority to make use of, rent out, or market the patented technologies. Because of these patents, the business has a competitive edge in the market and may offer distinctive software products and services that draw clients and make money.

Why Do We Need Different Types of Assets?

Different investment strategies, risk management, and financial goals all necessitate different kinds of assets. It is imperative to diversify one's assets among various categories for multiple reasons:

- ✓ **Risk mitigation**: The degree of risk attached to various asset classes varies. Individuals and investors can diversify their risk and lessen the impact of unfavorable events on their portfolios by holding a variety of assets. Bonds, for instance, could offer stability in the event that stock values decline.

- ✓ **Income Generation**: Certain investments, like dividend-paying stocks and bonds, provide a steady stream of income. These assets that generate income are essential for people who need the money to meet their financial objectives or pay for living expenses.

- ✓ **Capital Appreciation**: Over time, the value of assets like stocks and real estate may increase. Putting money into these kinds of assets has the potential to grow capital, raising the portfolio's total value.

- ✓ **Needs for Liquidity**: The amount of liquidity offered by various asset classes varies. When needed, liquid assets such as cash or money market funds can be quickly accessed. Possessing liquid assets guarantees that people can take advantage of investment opportunities or cover unforeseen costs.

- ✓ **Diversification**: Spreading investments over a variety of asset classes, including stocks, bonds, real estate, and more, is known as diversification. Portfolios with a variety of holdings can aid in striking a balance between return and risk. The volatility of the portfolio as a whole may be decreased when one asset class underperforms and is offset by others.

- ✓ **Financial Goals**: Various financial objectives call for varying asset allocations. Retirement savings, for instance, might entail a combination of income-producing assets like bonds and growth-oriented assets like stocks. Short-term objectives, such as vacation savings, might give priority to assets that are more liquid and stable.

- ✓ **Tax Efficiency**: The tax implications of various asset types vary. Tax efficiency and return impact can be reduced by using tax-advantaged accounts for certain assets, such as retirement savings in Individual Retirement Accounts (IRAs).

- ✓ **Inflation Hedging**: Commodities like gold and real estate are frequently regarded as inflation hedges. When the purchasing power of money is diminished by inflation, they may hold onto or even appreciate in value.

- ✓ **Long-Term vs. Short-Term needs**: People frequently have financial needs, both long-term and short-term. Various asset categories can be assigned according to the duration of those requirements. Growth-oriented assets can be included in long-term investments, whereas more liquid assets can be used to meet immediate needs.

- ✓ **Risk Tolerance**: The willingness and capacity of investors to tolerate market fluctuations is reflected in their varying levels of risk tolerance. In order to guarantee that a person can stick with their investment strategy and stay invested, asset allocation should be in line with their level of risk tolerance.

Building a Foundation of Assets

Unlocking your money power

Establishing a solid foundation of assets that generate income is the first step toward letting your assets pay for your luxuries. Here are some methods:

Invest in the stock market: Over time, dividends and capital gains can be obtained by purchasing stocks in reputable companies that are expanding. In particular, dividend-paying shares provide a regular profit stream.

Real estate: Owning condominiums can increase in value while also bringing in a monthly income. Another excellent option for those who would rather not manage properties directly are real estate investment trusts, or REITs.

Start a Side Business: A business, whether physical or virtual, has the potential to grow into a significant asset providing a consistent flow of revenue.

Intellectual Property: Produce something valuable that generates ongoing royalties, such as a book, patent, or digital content.

Walter Handerson

Make Money from Your hobbies and Passions: creating successful businesses out of what you love

Look into ways to make money from your interests, such as writing, music, crafting, or photography.

CONCLUSION

STAYING DETERMINED

When you first start your financial journey, it might be simple to stay motivated, but like any journey, there might be roadblocks that prevent you from moving forward and sap your motivation. Perhaps you've experienced a few unforeseen costs or financial errors. These small setbacks, though, don't have to determine how your financial plan turns out. Reaching your goals will inevitably bring you highs and lows, but staying motivated can be challenging. Here are some suggestions to assist you and others who are having trouble staying motivated financially.

- **Understand your why**

You may have heard that building credit or saving money are wise decisions. However, these chores can seem tiresome and boring if you don't understand why. Creating a motivation for completing specific financial tasks will give your financial journey some context. Your "why" may be to improve the quality of life for your future offspring, to purchase a house, or to be financially worry-free in retirement. Your "why" can serve as a powerful motivator to keep you focused, regardless of the reasons behind it.

- **Set SMART goals**.

When you are working toward a goal, it is much easier to stay motivated. Just like your "why," your goals can influence how you make financial decisions. Although the S.M.A.R.T. (Specific, Measurable, Achievable, Relevant, Time-bound) goal-setting technique is a good idea, these goals can be short- or long-term.

- **Maintain visual reminders about your goal or goals.**

Once your goals are clear, it's simple to monitor your daily progress toward achieving them. Make a goal thermometer or spreadsheet and post it somewhere you'll see it every day, like on your mirror or fridge. You always have a reminder of what you're aiming for when you visualize your goals. Saying no to pricey get-togethers with friends or impulsive purchases like new clothes or shoes can help you see the bigger picture.

- **Divide up more ambitious goals**

Even with the best of intentions and a goal you're excited to accomplish, larger, longer-term objectives, such as setting up an emergency fund, can seem overwhelming. Those objectives should be divided into more manageable milestones to prevent you from becoming overwhelmed in the long run. Your emergency reserve should cover three to six months' worth of living costs. This goal can be broken down into one-month intervals until it is met or surpassed. It's much less daunting to save enough money to last one month without a paycheck than it is to try to reach six or more months. Achieving several smaller objectives that culminate in a larger one can help you stay on track financially and enhance your mindset around money.

- **Celebrate wins (big or small)**

Remember to celebrate when you reach those checkpoints and break down your larger goals into their component parts. Part of your financial journey is deserving yourself a small reward every time you reach one of your goals. You should treat yourself to dessert at your preferred ice cream parlor if you succeeded in reaching your credit score target of over 700. Another financial accomplishment worth celebrating is paying off debt. Treat yourself to a bike, an easel, or other hobby item you could use on the weekends. Make sure that these small celebrations don't break the bank, but they can help you stay motivated.

- **Be in the company of positive people**.

It can start to wear on you if friends and family consistently put you in circumstances that negatively impact your finances and mental well-being. Try to surround yourself with people who support you in your financial endeavors whenever you can. These upbeat individuals will hold you responsible rather than stifle you. You can even start encouraging one another as you go through your individual financial journeys.

Unlocking your money power

- **Study up on the financial industry.**

Even though you think you know enough about money and everything related to it, you can always learn more. You can become a more knowledgeable financial person by reading a book or blog about investments and savings strategies, but you don't have to be a reader to become more financially savvy. Alternatively, you may subscribe to financial podcasts or view educational videos on the internet. You might decide as you gain more knowledge that you would like to increase your emergency fund or invest in a different retirement plan. Your objectives will probably shift and adjust as you gain more knowledge about various financial ideas.

- **Moving forward**

Progress doesn't always have to be linear, so you won't always be inspired and passionate. It's acceptable to experience setbacks along the journey. You are still moving in the right direction toward your objective of having a secure financial future as long as you don't make any significant mistakes. The best course of action is to keep going forward and concentrate on the current task at hand and **always speak positive words to yourself no**

matter what, the words we say goes a long way to keeping us motivated. Your enthusiasm and drive will return in spades once you've achieved your financial objective.

You should know more about how to maintain your enthusiasm for your finances during the entire process now that you've read these tips. These pointers will assist you in holding yourself responsible for your financial choices and better preparing you to handle both financial successes and setbacks. Recall that you can use your financial setback; whether it was from maxing out your credit cards, making the wrong investments, or simply reaching your lowest point—to spur yourself on to meet your financial objectives. To steer your financial ship toward and beyond your goals, you should strive to take a lesson from every financial setback and form new habits.

Remember, your future is in your hands.

Unlocking your money power

www.ingramcontent.com/pod-product-compliance
Lightning Source LLC
Chambersburg PA
CBHW071949210526
45479CB00003B/865